THE LITTLE BOOK OF

MANCHESTER UNITED LEGENDS

Independent and Unofficial

First published in 2025 by OH
An Imprint of HEADLINE PUBLISHING GROUP LIMITED

1

Disclaimer:

Cataloguing in Publication Data is available from the British Library

ISBN 978-1-03542-286-9

Compiled and written by: David Clayton
Editorial: Chris Stone and Matt Tomlinson
Designed and typset in Helvetica Now by: Tony Seddon
Project manager: Russell Porter
Production: Rachel Burgess
Printed and bound in Dubai

HEADLINE PUBLISHING GROUP LIMITED
An Hachette UK Company
Carmelite House, 50 Victoria Embankment, London EC4Y 0DZ

The authorised representative in the EEA is Hachette Ireland, 8 Castlecourt Centre, Dublin 15, D15 XTP3, Ireland (email: info@hbgi.ie)

www.headline.co.uk www.hachette.co.uk

THE LITTLE BOOK OF

MANCHESTER UNITED LEGENDS

Independent and Unofficial

THE GREATEST PLAYERS TO WEAR THE SHIRT
AND THE GREATEST MANGERS TO LEAD THE TEAM

CONTENTS

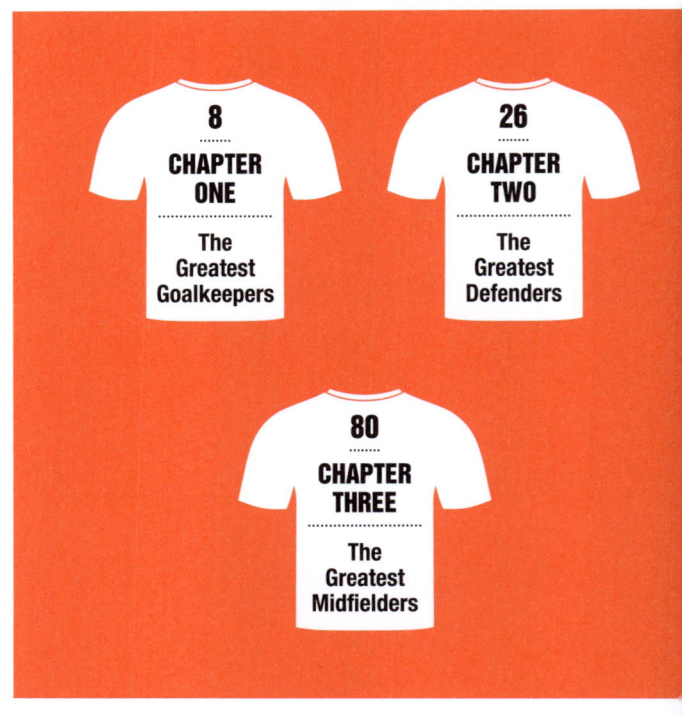

INTRODUCTION

Founded in 1878 as Newton Heath, the name Manchester United Football Club came into being in 1902. Not only would United become one of English football's biggest and most successful teams, they would go on to conquer Europe and arguably become the biggest and most famous club in world football.

With a fanbase that spreads far and wide across the globe, the Reds have experienced more success than most and have enjoyed many glorious eras, won countless trophies and many legends of the game have worn that famous red shirt over the years.

With 70 trophies won to date – including 20 top-flight titles and three Champions League successes – the Reds have been a dominant force during varying eras, most notably during the reign of Sir Alex Ferguson.

But there have been other glorious spells, including that of Sir Matt Busby and the entertaining – if brief – years of Tommy Docherty and Ron Atkinson.

The Old Trafford club have also known tragedy, with the Munich air disaster in 1958 claiming the lives of several of the so-called "Busby Babes".

United legends are numerous, from goalkeeping giants like Peter Schmeichel and David de Gea to defensive colossuses like Nemanja Vidić, Martin Buchan and Gary Pallister.

In midfield, there have been icons such as Bryan Robson, David Beckham and Roy Keane, while the forward line has included mesmeric talents such as Eric Cantona, Ryan Giggs and George Best.

In the pages that follow, you'll discover the players and managers that have lit up the Theatre of Dreams and remained in the memories of those lucky enough to have seen them. From the past and present, *The Little Book of Manchester United Legends* showcases the giants that have made this football club what it is today.

CHAPTER

1

THE GREATEST GOALKEEPERS

Being the Manchester United No. 1 carries great responsibility, and over the years several names have stood out – the four names in this chapter are the ones that have achieved legendary status.

Peter Schmeichel
1991 – 1999

It's difficult to imagine a more influential or imposing figure than Peter Schmiechel in his heyday. The Danish giant was absolutely key to many of United's successes during the 1990s, when he clocked up just shy of 400 appearances for the Reds.

Vocal, brash and brimming with confidence, Schmeichel was the last line of an already formidable United defence, and if ever a goalkeeper was born to play for Manchester United, it was Schmeichel. His role in the all-conquering United side of the 1990s cannot be understated – a giant in every sense of the word.

GAMES

League 292
FA Cup.................................41
League Cup 17
Europe................................ 42
Other................................... 6
Total............................**398**

TROPHIES

Premier League x 5
FA Cup x 3
League Cup x 1
FA Charity Shield x 4

Champions League x 1
UEFA Super Cup x 1

I don't believe a better goalkeeper played
the game. He is a giant figure in the history
of Manchester United.

SIR ALEX FERGUSON

Peter is a superb professional and was a
fantastic loyal servant to Manchester United.

SIR ALEX FERGUSON

Success is not about being the best, it's
about always getting better.

PETER SCHMEICHEL

Success is not measured by trophies, but
by the impact you have on others.

PETER SCHMEICHEL

Edwin van der Sar

2005 – 2011

If Peter Schmeichel is United's greatest goalkeeper of all time, Edwin van der Sar runs the Danish legend pretty close. After Schmeichel left in 1999, the Reds struggled to find a replacement with the same authority and dependability – until Van der Sar was signed in 2005.

Eyebrows were raised at the signature of a 34-year-old, but it proved to be an inspired signing, and for six years the Dutch keeper helped United maintain their domestic dominance and continue to challenge among Europe's elite. With 11 trophies during his time at Old Trafford, Van der Sar has earned his place among the legends of the club.

GAMES

League 186
FA Cup................................. 13
League Cup 5
Europe................................. 56
Other................................... 6
Total............................ **266**

TROPHIES

Premier League x 4
League Cup x 2
FA Community Shield x 3

Champions League x 1
FIFA Club World Cup x 1

He is not a normal keeper. The players in front of him always can have the thought: we still have Edwin. He has got so much talent and a strong character. Maybe he is the best goalkeeper United ever had, but we also had Schmeichel. But Van der Sar is unique.

SIR BOBBY CHARLTON

Edwin is the best goalkeeper we have had since Peter Schmeichel. He is a winner. He has brought with him a strength of character; he really looks after himself and he trains very well. There are many players who, having achieved what he has done, want to take it easy. But he has a desire to carry on. Edwin's professionalism and dedication to his job and the way he looks after himself has given him longevity in the game.

SIR ALEX FERGUSON

I get great respect from the United fans and the directors and the people who are there still when you go there. It is a very warm club, very comparable to Ajax, only they have grown internationally amazingly.

EDWIN VAN DER SAR

Saving the last penalty to win the Champions League in 2008 was the most unbelievable moment of my life.

EDWIN VAN DER SAR

David de Gea

2011 – 2023

Not only a Manchester United great, but one of the best goalkeepers the Premier League has ever seen, David de Gea kept the No. 1 jersey for the Reds for 12 years. Agile, dependable and a terrific shot-stopper, De Gea was unfortunate to keep goal during United's transitional period.

Throughout what was, at times, a turbulent period for the club, De Gea remained consistent and steadfast, often single-handedly winning games for the Reds during a decade-plus of excellence. He will be remembered fondly at Old Trafford for many years to come.

GAMES

League	415
FA Cup	28
League Cup	16
Europe	82
Other	4
Total	**545**

TROPHIES

Premier League x 1

FA Cup x 1

League Cup x 2

FA Community Shield x 3

Europa League x 1

I admire David de Gea. I cannot remember anyone coming into Manchester United and being criticised the way he was. He was the subject of every debate in the media. You haven't seen De Gea defend himself in the media or shifting the blame elsewhere. He just gets on with it.

PETER SCHMEICHEL

Dean (Henderson) has had a fantastic couple of years at Sheffield United and I think eventually he will end up as England No 1 and Man United No 1. But he's got the best goalkeeper in the world in David de Gea ahead of him and for me David is still developing, still getting better.

OLE GUNNAR SOLSKJÆR

"

You cannot train saving with your feet, but sometimes it is instinct. Sometimes it is quicker to go with the feet; going with the hands is sometimes more difficult. Even when I was young, I would go with my feet, it's something good for me.

"

DAVID DE GEA

"

I took incredible pride every time I pulled on this shirt – to lead the team, to represent this institution, the biggest club in the world – was an honour only bestowed upon a few lucky footballers.

"

DAVID DE GEA

Alex Stepney
1966 – 1978

One of United's longest serving players, Alex Stepney spent the best part of 12 years as the Reds' No. 1. Stepney experienced highs and lows during his career, with his performance in the 4–1 European Cup final win over Benfica in 1968 undoubtedly the pinnacle, and the 1974 relegation to Division Two the lowest ebb.

His appearance total bears testament to his reliability and longevity during a topsy-turvy period for the club, and though his trophy haul perhaps doesn't reflect his efforts, the respect he is held in by those who saw him play is reward enough for this most loyal United servant.

GAMES

League 430
FA Cup.................................. 45
League Cup 35
Europe................................. 25
Other..................................... 4
Total.............................. **539**

TROPHIES

First Division x 1
FA Cup x 1
FA Charity Shield x 2

European Cup x 1

The save he made from Eusebio in the
European Cup final was a great save.

SIR MATT BUSBY

And here's Eusebio! What a save from Stepney!
And what a sportsman, Eusebio when he could
have won that match, to applaud Stepney
like that.

KENNETH WOLSTENHOLME

We never spoke about Munich, it was an unwritten code, a 'no-no', but when the final whistle went we all knew what it meant. We all ran to Bobby [Charlton], Sir Matt Busby and Bill Foulkes as the emotion poured out, saying 'We've done it, we've done it.'

ALEX STEPNEY

On the 1968 European Cup triumph

Walking out at Wembley was a boyhood dream because back then you wanted to win the FA Cup and play for your country, and I had the honour of doing both.

ALEX STEPNEY

CHAPTER
2

THE GREATEST DEFENDERS

From the brave and bold to the fearless and fearsome, Manchester United have been blessed with some truly wonderful defenders. Warriors, commanders and tough-tacklers, here are some of the very best...

Martin Buchan

1972 – 1983

A defender ahead of his time, Martin Buchan was a classy, cool-headed central defender who almost broke the mould of the brawny centre-halves of his day.

The intelligent Scot arrived from Aberdeen and was soon skippering the Reds, and after suffering relegation, it was the cool head of Buchan that led United back to the top flight. He would go on to lift the FA Cup in 1977 and he helped United become a force to be reckoned with once more during his 11-year stay at Old Trafford.

GAMES and GOALS

League	376	4
FA Cup	39	0
League Cup	30	0
Europe	10	0
Other	1	0
Total	**456**	**4**

TROPHIES

FA Cup x 1

FA Charity Shield x 1

We were back at Manchester Town Hall on the Sunday, with the FA Cup this time, and I had it in my hands as we came off the bus. The main building was locked up, so I asked the Doc, 'What do I do with this?'

MARTIN BUCHAN

Take it home and bring it back in the morning.

TOMMY DOCHERTY

The exchange between Buchan and Manchester United boss Docherty at the 1977 FA Cup parade in central Manchester

I wasn't happy about relegation, but I decided to stay and help the club back into the First Division.

MARTIN BUCHAN

I well remember standing next to the Doc on the balcony of Manchester Town Hall when he told a packed Albert Square we would 'go back and win it next year'.

MARTIN BUCHAN

Gordon McQueen

1978 – 1985

When United convinced Gordon McQueen to swap Leeds United for the red half of Manchester in February 1978, the transfer created a seismic reaction on either side of the Pennines.

McQueen – a strapping Scottish centre-half – was arguably one of the most commanding defenders of the day and his capture was a major statement by the Reds. Few strikers enjoyed playing against McQueen, who was a towering presence in the air and a powerful force on the ground. His eight-year stay at Old Trafford also yielded a more-than-acceptable goal every eight games – almost always a header!

GAMES and GOALS

League	184	20
FA Cup	19	1
League Cup	9	4
Europe	7	0
Other	1	0
Total	**220**	**25**

TROPHIES

FA Cup x 1

FA Charity Shield x 1

He was a perfect fit for Manchester United with his flair, courage and big personality, and that's why the fans loved him. Most importantly, though, he was a brilliant person with a huge heart. He lit up any room he walked into.

BRYAN ROBSON

Gordon was the biggest character in football, large as life, funny, full of desire. Took to United like a natural and loved the roar after one of his runs.

LOU MACARI

99 per cent of players want to play for
Manchester United and the rest are liars.

GORDON MCQUEEN

Most of my playing contemporaries came from
the tough council estates. It was a harder life
which prepared me for what's happened.

GORDON MCQUEEN

Gary Neville

1992 – 2011

With 21 major titles, 602 games and 19 years' service, Gary Neville is one of the greatest and most successful Manchester United players of all time.

A steady, if not spectacular, right-back, Neville was one of the first names on the team-sheet for Sir Alex Ferguson – the only manager one-club-man Neville ever played under. He may not have scored or assisted many goals, but he was a vital cog in the most successful United side of all time, skippering the club for several years. A glorious career for the boyhood Red who got to live out his boyhood dreams.

GAMES and GOALS

League	400	5
FA Cup	47	0
League Cup	25	0
Europe	117	2
Other	13	0
Total	**602**	**7**

TROPHIES

Premier League x 8

FA Cup x 3

League Cup x 3

FA Charity/Community Shield x 3

Champions League x 2

Intercontinental Cup x 1

FIFA Club World Cup x 1

Gary was the best English right-back
of his generation.

SIR ALEX FERGUSON

He had a wonderful hunger and desire to
succeed, which kept him where he was in
the game... a Manchester United icon.

STEVE BRUCE

I have been a Manchester United fan all my life and fulfilled every dream I've ever had.

GARY NEVILLE

I developed a mechanism so that whatever mistakes I made, I would bounce straight back. Whatever was happening off the pitch, I could put it to one side and maintain my form. Call it mental resilience or a strong mind, but that is what we mean when we talk about experience in a football team.

GARY NEVILLE

Denis Irwin
1990 – 2002

United's Mr Reliable for more than a decade, Denis Irwin was the perfect left-back to match Gary Neville on the right. But whereas Neville rarely scored or assisted, Irwin would regularly chip in with goals, was excellent from set-pieces and assisted many goals for his team-mates.

It was Irwin's consistency that set him apart from most of his contemporaries, and his stay spanned two great United teams during his 12 years at Old Trafford. Irwin would clock up more than 500 appearances for the Reds during a glorious spell, collecting 18 winners medals along the way.

GAMES and GOALS

League 368 22
FA Cup..................... 43 7
League Cup 31 0
Europe..................... 75 4
Other...................... 12 0
Total................. **529** **33**

TROPHIES

Premier League x 7
FA Cup x 2
League Cup x 1
FA Charity Shield x 4

Champions League x 1
European Cup Winners' Cup x 1
UEFA Super Cup x 1
Intercontinental Cup x 1

We always called him Eight Out of Ten Denis.
So quick and nimble: quick-brained. Never let you
down. There was never any bad publicity with him.

SIR ALEX FERGUSON

You're talking about the modern full-back.
Denis could play at left-back, right-back, could
score a goal, good at set-pieces, very rarely
injured, good personality.

ROY KEANE

Nothing can top the 1999 Manchester United team – but our '94 side was such a joy to play in.

DENIS IRWIN

I went in and just got about my job. I wasn't a star player, but Fergie still appreciated me. I didn't cause him too much stress. My peers appreciated what I did, too. Maybe to the fan in the street I didn't make headlines because I wasn't a star player, but I didn't want the limelight.

DENIS IRWIN

Jaap Stam
1998 – 2001

Jaap Stam's Manchester United story is not perhaps what it could or should have been. A superb man-mountain of a defender, Stam was signed for a world record fee in 1998 and would prove to be the missing link of Sir Alex Ferguson's all-conquering side that would go on to win the treble in his first full season.

After another title in his second year, injuries hampered Stam's remaining time with the Reds, and when Lazio came in for his services, he was surprisingly allowed to leave. A short stay but a hugely impactful one, nonetheless.

GAMES and GOALS

League	79	1
FA Cup	8	0
League Cup	0	0
Europe	32	0
Other	8	0
Total	**127**	**1**

TROPHIES

Premier League x 3
FA Cup x 1

Champions League x 1
Intercontinental Cup x 1

At the time he had just come back from an Achilles injury, and we thought he had just lost a little bit. We got the offer from Lazio, £16.5m for a centre-back who was 29. It was an offer I couldn't refuse. But in playing terms it was a mistake. He is still playing for Ajax at a really good level.

SIR ALEX FERGUSON

Once Jaap's pace took him into the channel ahead of an attacking player they had no chance. He was so strong it was a mismatch. He would not be beaten.

RYAN GIGGS

I have always been a Manchester United supporter since I was a child, so that won't change.

JAAP STAM

We didn't give many goals away, we could see that opponents looked frightened when they came to Old Trafford. They might give it a go at the start of the game but then revert to drop deeper. We'd push and push. We didn't create loads of opportunities, but we always created enough to win games and we had players up front to finish them.

JAAP STAM

Nemanja Vidić
2006 – 2014

Quite simply, Nemanja Vidić was one of – if not the – best central defenders to ever represent the club. Relatively unknown when he joined from Spartak Moscow in 2006, everybody in English football knew him by the time his tenure at Old Trafford ended – and most long before.

The imposing Serbian was the rock of a United side that swept all before them, and his haul of winner's medals is testament to how good the Reds were when he was in the team. A modern-day legend in every sense of the word.

GAMES and GOALS

League	211	15
FA Cup	18	0
League Cup	11	1
Europe	52	3
Other	8	2
Total	**300**	**21**

TROPHIES

Premier League x 5
League Cup x 3
FA Community Shield x 5

Champions League x 1
FIFA Club World Cup x 1

Nemanja has made a terrific impact at the club. He has forged a partnership with Rio Ferdinand that was a major part in us winning the title last year [2006–07]. He is an extremely popular member of the squad, both with staff and fans alike. It's great news that he wants to be part of this exciting side for years to come.

SIR ALEX FERGUSON

Just talking about Nemanja, off the pitch he was fairly quiet. But on the pitch, in training, that guy was a scary bloke, honestly.

BEN FOSTER

Playing in this team is a great privilege. The fans and everyone at the club have been very special to me. I hope I can do my bit to bring the club even more trophies in the years ahead.

NEMANJA VIDIĆ

I'm not considering staying in England as the only club I ever wanted to play for here is Manchester United. I never could have imagined winning 15 trophies. However, I have decided I will move on at the end of this season.

NEMANJA VIDIĆ

Rio Ferdinand
2002 – 2014

A classy, fast and powerful central defender, Rio Ferdinand had it all. Alongside Nemanja Vidić, he formed a partnership that helped United dominate English football for the best part of a decade, with his polished, composed style setting him apart from many traditional No. 5s.

Intelligent and a great reader of the game, he was the right man at the right time for United, and his six Premier League titles are evidence enough of his importance to the team. He was signed for what was a world-record fee by the Reds – but he proved to be worth every penny and much more during his time at Old Trafford.

GAMES and GOALS

League	312	7
FA Cup	30	0
League Cup	14	0
Europe	91	1
Other	8	0
Total	**455**	**8**

TROPHIES

Premier League x 6
League Cup x 2
FA Community Shield x 4

Champions League x 1
FIFA Club World Cup x 1

He was a great player, without a doubt the best centre-half I ever played with. I would say for a time as well he was the best centre-half in the world. He was such a pleasure to play with and play in front of. To play in front of him, he made your job so easy.

PAUL SCHOLES

What a player he was: absolute Rolls-Royce.

MICHAEL OWEN

Circumstances didn't allow for me to say goodbye the way I would have liked but I'd like to take this opportunity to thank my team-mates, staff, the club and the fans for an unbelievable 12 years that I'll never forget.

RIO FERDINAND

Winning trophies over my 12 years at Manchester United allowed me to achieve everything that I desired in football. From a young child to today, that was all I cared about. None of that would have been possible without the genius of one man: Sir Alex Ferguson. His greatest accomplishment in my eyes will always be how he developed us as men, not just as footballers. He will, in my opinion, always be the greatest manager in British football history.

RIO FERDINAND

Roger Byrne

1951 – 1958

Roger Byrne was a defender who made up for any deficiencies in his game through sheer hard work and intelligence. The general view was that he wasn't the best tackler and wasn't so good in the air, but he was very much a left-back ahead of his time, relying instead on intelligence, an innate gift for sniffing out danger and being able to cut it out accordingly.

Byrne also enjoyed attacking down the flank in a time when defenders defended and did little else. Matt Busby made him captain and the Reds would go on to win successive titles before he was tragically killed in the Munich air disaster aged 28.

GAMES and GOALS

League	245	17
FA Cup	18	2
League Cup	0	0
Europe	14	0
Other	3	1
Total	**280**	**20**

TROPHIES

First Division x 3

FA Charity Shield x 3

Here was the captain courageous – a strong man who listened to the crowd's boos and heard a call to action... who listened to two stern lectures from the referee and charged back into the game as if they had been pep talks. This was the moment when Byrne stepped in, the longer they booed, the harder he played. He loved it!

UNCREDITED MATCH REPORT, 1956

My dad was an only child and was doted on so his loss hit his parents hard. Grandad took me to all the Manchester United games and talked about dad all the time. His grief was tempered by immense pride, and I grew up as proud of dad as he was.

ROGER BYRNE JR

Roger would talk about football constantly. He loved the game. Of course, he was a tremendous player and I'm sure he'd have gone to the World Cup in the summer of 1958. He wasn't the most vocal captain – instead he led by example. He had great presence on the pitch, and we all looked up to him immensely. If you did well, you would not expect more than a pat on the back. Yet from Roger, it was a gesture you would prize very highly.

SIR BOBBY CHARLTON

I don't remember Roger making too many tackles. He didn't need to because he read the game so well. And he had tremendous pace! He was admired and I've no doubt he would have captained England.

WILF MCGUINNESS

Bill Foulkes
1951 – 1970

Bill Foulkes' Manchester United story is one mixed with triumph and tragedy. Foulkes was a survivor of the Munich air crash in 1958, and 10 years later, a member of the side that won the European Cup. The Busby Babe was an uncompromising centre-back, renowned for his tough tackling, no-nonsense style.

He would – for a time – become United's record appearance holder and is fourth of all time today. His determination to see the Reds become the champions of Europe was partly driven by the memory of those lost in the plane crash and what they might have become. A true Manchester United legend.

GAMES and GOALS

League	566	7
FA Cup	61	0
League Cup	3	0
Europe	52	2
Other	6	0
Total	**688**	**9**

TROPHIES

First Division x 4
FA Cup x 1
FA Charity Shield x 3

European Cup x 1

He was as hard as nails, as tough as teak. I was always glad I didn't have to play against him.

SIR BOBBY CHARLTON

Bill was a giant character. He was a very gentle man, who I was privileged to meet on several occasions, including most memorably with his team-mates at the Champions League final in Moscow, 50 years after his heroics in the Munich air crash.

ED WOODWARD

ex-Vice Chairman

It was obvious that we would struggle to take off and they took the chance. They should never have done that. I don't feel guilty about being a survivor. I was just damned lucky. But I do harbour this feeling that it wasn't necessary, that angers me. It cost the club, it cost the country so much.

BILL FOULKES

I don't think the Busby years can ever be eclipsed. They built the legend. We had three European Players of the Year in George Best, Denis Law and Bobby Charlton in the same side. I can't see that happening again.

BILL FOULKES

Gary Pallister
1989 – 1998

When United paid Middlesbrough a British record fee to bring the highly rated Gary Pallister to Old Trafford, a few eyebrows were raised. Could the 23-year-old centre-back handle the change and thrive in the spotlight? Some nine years and 15 trophies later, everyone had their answer.

The towering defender was a superb acquisition that was a key part of United's domestic dominance of the 1990s and an imposing figure for opposition attackers. An intelligent and skilful player, his partnership with Steve Bruce at the heart of the Reds' defence was also one of the best for many years and Pallister's penchant for important goals also enhanced his reputation.

GAMES and GOALS

League	317	12
FA Cup	38	2
League Cup	36	0
Europe	41	1
Other	5	0
Total	**437**	**15**

TROPHIES

Premier League x 4

FA Cup x 3

League Cup x 1

FA Charity Shield x 5

European Cup Winners' Cup x 1

UEFA Super Cup x 1

Gary has enjoyed a fantastic career as one of the game's best defenders with Middlesbrough, Manchester United and England.

STEVE McCLAREN

He is a defensive Goliath, has electric pace and can pass the ball.

SIR ALEX FERGUSON

To win the league after 26 years was amazing. I think you had to be in Old Trafford that night when we picked up the Premier League trophy. We were already crowned champions the night before we played Blackburn in '93, but to walk into the stadium that night, you realised what it meant to play for Manchester United or to be a Manchester United fan.

GARY PALLISTER

My relationship with the gaffer was pretty good. You're always a little bit wary of Sir Alex and when he had his moments and you were in a firing line, it wasn't a nice place to be. But my relationship with the gaffer was great.

GARY PALLISTER

Nobby Stiles
1960 – 1971

Nobby Stiles started out life as a full-back before being converted into a defensive midfielder by Matt Busby. The diminutive Mancunian more than made up for his lack of height with heart and courage. Stiles was a ferocious opponent, with a desire to win the ball illustrated in his famed crunching tackles.

The balding, toothless (front top at least!), short-sighted and small Stiles might have looked anything but a footballer, but for a decade he prowled the area just in front of United's defence. He famously was part of the England side that won the World Cup in 1966 and his spontaneous jig holding the Jules Rimet trophy remains one of the most memorable moments in English football.

GAMES and GOALS

League	311	17
FA Cup	38	0
League Cup	7	0
Europe	36	2
Other	3	0
Total	**395**	**19**

TROPHIES

First Division x 2

FA Cup x 1

FA Charity Shield x 2

European Cup x 1

We can dance Nobby's dance,
we can dance it in France.

DAVID BADDIEL & FRANK SKINNER

He was a very demanding team-mate.
He expected you to produce, he didn't
mollycoddle you.

BRIAN KIDD

It was not so much a triumph for our football club as the blood of our lives. We were kids when the Busby Babes were wiped out and we had felt the sorrow on the streets of our city.

NOBBY STILES

On the 1968 European Cup win

Nobby, I want you to take Eusebio out of the game...

SIR ALF RAMSEY

England manager, before the 1966 World Cup semi-final game against Portugal

... Do you mean for good, Alf?

NOBBY STILES

Patrice Evra
2006 – 2014

It took eight years for Patrice Evra to catch the attention of top clubs in Europe after stints with various clubs in Italy and France. It was with Monaco that his potential really came to the fore, and when he learned of Manchester United's interest, there was only one club he wanted to play for.

Evra took to Sir Alex Ferguson's side like the proverbial duck to water, with his dynamic bursts of pace from left-back adding an additional bow to a team already full of attacking talent. Evra was the right man at the right time and he loved every minute of being a United player, and it showed each and every time he pulled on that red shirt.

GAMES and GOALS

League	273	7
FA Cup	20	0
League Cup	11	1
Europe	67	2
Other	8	0
Total	**379**	**10**

TROPHIES

Premier League x 5
League Cup x 3
FA Community Shield x 4

Champions League x 1
FIFA Club World Cup x 1

I've always been blessed with a good memory but Patrice Evra? There's a man with a brain. He could speak five languages and was a great help in the dressing room. Lovely guy. His father was a diplomat, it showed.

SIR ALEX FERGUSON

He knows the football club inside out. He's a good lad to have in the dressing room, a good leader and a bubbly character.

DENIS IRWIN

I love Man United, and I will always love Man United. It is not a fake love.

PATRICE EVRA

I know the city and the club, and I can tell you that when you play for Manchester United at Old Trafford, you no longer need to see the sunshine every day.

PATRICE EVRA

Steve Bruce
1987 – 1996

One half of what many consider to have been United's best ever central defensive partnership, Steve Bruce (along with Gary Pallister) gave his all for the Reds during a successful nine-year stay. Bruce helped end United's 26-year wait to become the champions of England again, and he was a powerful, no-nonsense defender.

Excellent in the air and perhaps underrated with the ball at his feet, Bruce typified the spirit of a resurgent United side and was one of Sir Alex Ferguson's leaders on the pitch, who also regularly chipped in with vital goals.

GAMES and GOALS

League	309	36
FA Cup	41	3
League Cup	34	6
Europe	27	6
Other	3	1
Total	**414**	**51**

TROPHIES

Premier League x 3

FA Cup x 3

League Cup x 1

FA Charity Shield x 3

European Cup Winners' Cup x 1

UEFA Super Cup x 1

Brucey was the captain of the club, he lifted trophies, played with his heart on his sleeve, gave everything he had for United.

GARY PALLISTER

When he was playing for me at Manchester United, I observed that he always had a fantastic ability to communicate and motivate.

SIR ALEX FERGUSON

I'll never forget the first time walking into the dressing room with Whiteside and McGrath and Robson and Strachan and Olsen, and these people. [I was] thinking, I've only just seen these on the telly before, you know, and now I'm trying to kick a ball with them. I remember watching Paul McGrath thinking, Am I really going to take over from him? God, what a player he is!

STEVE BRUCE

Of course, nothing takes you from the step from Norwich to Man United. Man United was the biggest one of all but I was determined after the 10 years I'd had was [that] I'm going to try to enjoy this. This has got to be the ultimate.

STEVE BRUCE

CHAPTER
3

THE GREATEST MIDFIELDERS

Playing in midfield for Manchester United carries a great weight of expectation given some of the names who have played in this position for the Reds over the years. From Duncan Edwards to David Beckham – here are some of the finest examples...

Paul Scholes

1994 – 2013

If you are looking for a Manchester United legend who pretty much had it all, look no further than Paul Scholes. Scholes spent his entire career with the Reds, accumulating the third-most appearances in the process.

Scholes had a bit of everything – a superb passer, excellent vision and the ability to score wonderful goals. He was the beating heart of two magnificent eras for the Reds and without doubt one of the club's all-time greats. With 25 major trophies in his career, Scholes sits comfortably among a pantheon of Manchester United legends.

GAMES and GOALS

League	499	107
FA Cup	49	13
League Cup	21	9
Europe	134	26
Other	15	0
Total	**718**	**155**

TROPHIES

Premier League x 11

FA Cup x 3

League Cup x 2

FA Charity /Community Shield x 5

Champions League x 2

Intercontinental Cup x 1

FIFA Club World Cup x 1

Everyone of us should emulate him.
We can all learn from Paul Scholes.

PETER SCHMEICHEL

There was never any question about Scholesy's
quality as a footballer. He was known as the little
ginger magician in the youth team. Some reckon
he's the best United player of the modern era, and
there's a case for saying that. You don't hear him
blowing his own trumpet, though – he just gets on
with his job. He's the real deal.

STEVE BRUCE

I don't like compliments. No. I prefer criticisms; prefer to prove them wrong.

PAUL SCHOLES

Get up. Go to work. Play the game.
Get showered. Go home.

PAUL SCHOLES

Bryan Robson
1981 – 1994

United's very own Captain Marvel, Bryan Robson was a dynamic, all-action and inspirational captain who helped change the culture at Old Trafford from winning the occasional cup competition to serial Premier League winners.

Robson left everything on the pitch and was a fantastic leader who helped bring the best out of those around him. He'd been at Old Trafford for almost 12 years when the Reds finally were crowned champions in 1993 – a first success in 26 years – and helped lay the foundation for the many titles that followed. An all-time great.

GAMES and GOALS

League	345	74
FA Cup	35	10
League Cup	51	5
Europe	27	8
Other	7	2
Total	**461**	**99**

TROPHIES

Premier League x 2

FA Cup x 3

FA Charity Shield x 2

European Cup Winners' Cup x 1

What Bobby Charlton was to my father,
Bryan Robson was to me – and still is. But
Bryan, as well as being great going forward,
could tackle and he could defend. I could
never do either of those things.

DAVID BECKHAM

When Robson plays football, he must
expect to get hurt, because that's him.
When he sees a ball, irrespective of where it
is on a football field, he automatically goes
for it. Afterwards, he sometimes says, 'I
don't really know why I went for it.' And he'll
be asking that when he's lying in the
treatment room. But that is Robson, and
that is the end of the story with him.

BRIAN CLOUGH

Winning the Championship is like taking a 26-year ball and chain from around our legs. Now we can go forward and hopefully dominate English football for the next 10 years, like Liverpool did.

BRYAN ROBSON

In a way, certain sections of the media always wanted to knock me because I had captained my country and been skipper at Old Trafford. It was all a bit odd really.

BRYAN ROBSON

Roy Keane
1993 – 2005

Roy Keane has to be considered as one of Manchester United's best pound-for-pound signings of all-time – but it could have been so different. Blackburn Rovers had agreed a fee with Nottingham Forest and Keane was all set to sign for the Lancashire club, but an administration error opened the door for the Reds, who nipped in to pay a British record £3.75m for the Irish midfielder.

Keane would go on to become an icon at Old Trafford, and with his imposing physicality, thundering challenges and leadership, he was the perfect replacement for the ageing Bryan Robson. A magnificent – and at times ferocious – servant for Manchester United.

GAMES and GOALS

League	326	33
FA Cup	46	2
League Cup	14	0
Europe	82	14
Other	12	2
Total	**480**	**51**

TROPHIES

Premier League x 7

FA Cup x 4

FA Charity/Community Shield x 4

Champions League x 1

Intercontinental Cup x 1

"

He looked like a Manchester United player as soon as I saw him. We played him at Forest and the way he played told me a lot about the lad. His determination, his energy, his attitude to losing and winning told me something about him before we even got him. With Roy Keane present, keeping the ball was never a problem.

"

SIR ALEX FERGUSON

"

He was a great player, beyond question. A midfielder of extraordinary tenacity and box-to-box dynamism, with a ferocious tackle and an underrated ability to use the ball astutely. But perhaps his greatest gift was to create a standard of performance which demanded the very best from his team. There wasn't a player at United who could match Roy's influence in my time at the club.

"

GARY NEVILLE

I loved Old Trafford from the moment
I set foot in it.

ROY KEANE

I found it difficult to cope with the kind of
fame that accompanied my status as a
footballer. You could describe this as the
Greta Garbo Syndrome. I wanted to be alone.

ROY KEANE

David Beckham

1992 – 2003

Perhaps one of Manchester United's most famous players of all time, David Beckham was always destined for greatness. From the moment he scored direct from a corner while on loan with Preston to the spectacular effort he scored against Wimbledon from the halfway line in 1996, Beckham's star was on a continual rise.

A brilliant set-piece taker and wonderful crosser and passer, Beckham was the golden boy of the famed Class of '92 batch of youngsters who helped the Reds become a powerhouse of English football for the first time in 26 years. A boyhood Red, Beckham achieved all his dreams at Old Trafford, and much more.

GAMES and GOALS

League	265	62
FA Cup	24	6
League Cup	12	1
Europe	83	15
Other	10	1
Total	**394**	**85**

TROPHIES

Premier League x 6
FA Cup x 2
FA Charity Shield x 2

Champions League x 1
Intercontinental Cup x 1

I don't know how he manages to be so at ease
outwardly on the pitch. He is almost a pop star.
I couldn't do that. It is incredible, especially
given that he is as timid as me.

ZINEDINE ZIDANE

From the start you knew the quality he had and
the professionalism. His range of passing and his
free kicks were brilliant and that was no accident
– he was out there practising all day long.

PAUL SCHOLES

I have always believed that if you want to
achieve anything special in life you have to
work, work, and then work some more.

DAVID BECKHAM

With United, we'd all grown up together, we
all wanted to win the biggest trophy in football.
We did it together.

DAVID BECKHAM

Bruno Fernandes

2020 – present day

A gifted box-to-box attacking midfielder, Bruno Fernandes has been unlucky in that he's been in a United side that has largely struggled to compete for the biggest prizes since he joined from Sporting Lisbon. The captain of the side, he has sometimes been criticised for wearing his heart on his sleeve and allowing his emotions to surface, but few could doubt his ability and desire.

Capable of superb goals, wonderful assists and breathtaking skill, Fernandes has been a terrific signing for the Reds, with perhaps his best years still to come.

GAMES and GOALS*

League	180	59
FA Cup	21	9
League Cup	13	4
Europe	51	16
Other	1	0
Total	**266**	**88**

as of 31/01/2025

TROPHIES

FA Cup x 1

League Cup x 1

Bruno's goals and assists stats speak for themselves. He will be a fantastic addition to our team, and he will help us push on in the second part of the season. Most importantly, he is a terrific human being with a great personality and his leadership qualities are clear for all to see.

OLE GUNNAR SOLSKJÆR

This guy's creativity is one of the best I've ever seen.

PEP GUARDIOLA

We have to go into every game with the same mentality as we have for Liverpool. It can be different playing against Burnley to Liverpool. I understand for the fans it's different but, for us, it can't be because the result we want is the same and nothing else.

BRUNO FERNANDES

For me, ever since I was a kid, it was a dream playing for Manchester United.

BRUNO FERNANDES

Paul Ince

1989 – 1995

Energetic, athletic, feisty and dynamic, Paul Ince was all this and more. His partnership with Bryan Robson helped the Reds to a first Premier League title in 26 years and when Robson left, it was Ince and Roy Keane who forged a formidable central midfield for the Reds that would result in many trophies.

His six seasons at Old Trafford were not without controversy and he had a major falling out with Sir Alex Ferguson, but while he wore the red shirt, he gave his all and was integral in helping turn around the club's fortunes.

GAMES and GOALS

League	206	25
FA Cup	27	1
League Cup	24	2
Europe	20	0
Other	4	1
Total	**281**	**29**

TROPHIES

Premier League x 2
FA Cup x 2
League Cup x 1
FA Charity Shield x 3

European Cup Winners' Cup x 1
UEFA Super Cup x 1

There's only one guv'nor around here
Incey, and it ain't you.

SIR ALEX FERGUSON

When he was at United, there was all this talk of
Incey being 'The Guv'nor', and people held that
against him. That was just banter. No nastiness
with that. Incey was a really good team-mate,
and a very good player.

ROY KEANE

When I first went to United, my idol was Bryan Robson, so I wanted to play with him. To get that last season – in 1992–93 – with Robson was amazing.

PAUL INCE

Me and Keaney, after every game – whether we'd won, lost or drawn – we used to sit down in the changing room when everyone had gone and analyse our performances.

PAUL INCE

Nicky Butt
1992 – 2004

Perhaps the least celebrated of the Class of '92, Nicky Butt's contribution was no less than some of the youngsters he grew up with, and he became integral to Manchester United's almost unparalleled domination of domestic football.

Butt was happy to stay out of the limelight and do the "dirty work" – breaking up play, winning the ball back and then giving it to more technically blessed team-mates. The fact he was a mainstay in a side that won six Premier League titles is evidence enough of his importance to the club.

GAMES and GOALS

League	270	21
FA Cup	29	1
League Cup	8	0
Europe	71	2
Other	9	2
Total	**387**	**26**

TROPHIES

Premier League x 6

FA Cup x 3

FA Charity/Community Shield x 4

Champions League x 1

Intercontinental Cup x 1

I always remember when we were in trouble at times at United, Sir Alex would put Nicky Butt in midfield with Roy Keane.

GARY NEVILLE

Nicky will always be a legend of Manchester United as a six-time Premier League winner.

OLE GUNNAR SOLSKJÆR

The local rivalry, the build-up of a derby game –
when you've been brought up in the area and you're
a Man United fan, you can't really describe what it
feels like. I remember getting up on the day of a
derby – up at 7am and the atmosphere around
the area is just brilliant.

NICKY BUTT

I remember when I was leaving [Man] United, when I
knew it was time to leave, I got asked to join [Man]
City off Stuart Pearce, he rang me up. I said, 'I'll have
a think about it', but I knew 'no, it can't happen'. I just
wanted to get him off the phone, to be fair. There
was no way I was going because of my dynamic in
my house. My family life would have been… I'm
alright. I'm out the way, but my brother and all that…
It would have been a nightmare. I would never have
been able to play for City.

NICKY BUTT

Norman Whiteside

1982 – 1989

Manchester United's very own wonderkid, Norman Whiteside burst into the first team aged 16 – breaking Duncan Edwards' record – and was captaining the side aged 20. He broke Pelé's record of being the youngest player to represent his country at the World Cup and he scored the winning goal in the 1985 FA Cup final.

An explosive talent, Whiteside should have gone on to become one of the club's greatest players, but a knee injury that today would have required simple keyhole surgery took its toll on the Northern Irish midfielder. He eventually left for Everton aged 24 and was forced to retire just two years later.

GAMES and GOALS

League	206	47
FA Cup	24	10
League Cup	29	9
Europe	13	1
Other	2	0
Total	**274**	**67**

TROPHIES

FA Cup x 2

FA Charity Shield x 1

If Norman had a yard more pace he would have been one of the greatest players ever produced in British football.

SIR ALEX FERGUSON

He would be classed, certainly, as a Busby Babe in the old sense. We had really skilful young players that suddenly had to play with men, and that's what Norman Whiteside has done.

SIR BOBBY CHARLTON

The only thing I have in common with George Best is that we came from the same place, play for the same club and were discovered by the same man.

NORMAN WHITESIDE

Sir Matt put his arm around me and said, 'We're hearing great things about you, we'll look after you. Enjoy your time at Manchester United.'

NORMAN WHITESIDE

Recalling his flight from Belfast to Manchester and his visit to Old Trafford as a 13-year-old for his trial

Sammy McIlroy

1971 – 1982

For more than a decade, the sight of a bustling all-action Sammy McIlroy was synonymous with Manchester United. The Northern Irish midfielder was Sir Matt Busby's final signing and broke into the side during a turbulent time that would end in relegation to the second tier in 1974.

The hard-working McIlroy was at the forefront of the Reds' resurgence, rarely missing a game and chipping in with a decent return of goals each season, as well as making many others for his team-mates. He excelled during what was a decade that proved rarely dull and left his mark at Old Trafford.

GAMES and GOALS

League	342	57
FA Cup	38	6
League Cup	28	6
Europe	10	2
Other	1	0
Total	**419**	**71**

TROPHIES

Division Two x 1

FA Cup x 1

FA Charity Shield x 1

Did you know?

On 6 November 1971 Sammy McIlroy made an unforgettable Manchester United debut against local rivals Manchester City.

Not only did he score in the 3-3 draw, he also set up the other two goals for his team-mates.

"

Monday morning George [Best] brought the champagne in, we were playing Stoke City in the League Cup that night and we met at Old Trafford and had a photograph of George giving me the bottle of champagne. I didn't have the guts to tell him I didn't like champagne, but because it came from George I kept it for years!

"

SAMMY McILROY

George was one of the main reasons why I went there, just as a young boy back in Belfast watching him play on the black and white televisions. Once I saw George play then after school I'd be in the streets trying to do the things he was doing. He was one of the main reasons that I wanted to play for United.

"

SAMMY McILROY

Michael Carrick
2006 – 2018

Humble, diligent and talented, Michael Carrick's name might not be mentioned in the same breath as some of United's more celebrated names of recent years, but his contribution is equal to almost all his contemporaries.

With 464 appearances and 18 major trophies, Carrick's 12-year stay at Old Trafford was an unqualified success and the cultured midfielder, who was happy to drop into the back four when required, was a calming presence in a Reds team that was on something of a rollercoaster ride during his time at the club. A manager's dream, he is now transferring his attributes into his own promising management career – as his brief role as caretaker boss at United in 2021 suggested it might.

GAMES and GOALS

League 316 17
FA Cup....................... 35 1
League Cup 19 2
Europe....................... 86 4
Other........................... 8 0
Total................. **464** **24**

TROPHIES

Premier League x 5
FA Cup x 1
League Cup x 3
FA Community Shield x 6

Champions League x 1
Europa League x 1
FIFA Club World Cup x 1

I think Michael's the best central midfielder in English football. I think he's the best English player in the game.

SIR ALEX FERGUSON

Scholes and Carrick together was peaceful. It was like going into a bar and hearing a piano playing. It's relaxing.

GARY NEVILLE

When I came in at United, I'd seen what the manager set, how the players lived their lives, how they trained, how they lived with the expectation and all sorts, playing three games a week at that level. And that is when I thought, Woah – this is different, this is something else.

MICHAEL CARRICK

Some lads were dribblers, some lads just loved scoring goals, whereas I enjoyed and took pride in practising my passing and that. That's how it was.

MICHAEL CARRICK

Duncan Edwards

1953 – 1958

Widely regarded as the greatest Manchester United player of all time, we can only guess just how good Duncan Edwards would have become. The Reds' coveted midfielder was just 21 when he lost his life in the Munich air disaster yet had already made a huge impact since his debut as a 17-year-old. Bobby Charlton described him as 'the best player I have ever seen'.

The two-footed Edwards had it all – he was physically strong and imposing, dynamic on the ball and he could pass a ball as well as any before or since. At the time of his death, he'd already helped United to two league titles, played 177 games and represented England 18 times. An incredible talent.

GAMES and GOALS

League	151	20
FA Cup	12	1
League Cup	0	0
Europe	12	0
Other	2	0
Total	**177**	**21**

TROPHIES

First Division x 2

FA Charity Shield x 2

George Best was something special, as was Pelé and Maradona, but in my mind Duncan was much better in terms of all-round ability and skill.

TOMMY DOCHERTY

Duncan was the best player in the world. He was without side, swagger, airs or graces.

SIR MATT BUSBY

Duncan tackled like a lion, attacked at every opportunity and topped it off with that cracker of a goal. He was still only 19, but already a world-class player.

BILLY WRIGHT

Even if you are having a nightmare day during which nothing will go right, never cease looking for the ball. In the end everything will come right, for football is a game that rewards those who show courage.

DUNCAN EDWARDS

CHAPTER
4

THE GREATEST FORWARDS

To say Manchester United has been blessed with some of the greatest forwards to have graced the game is not an understatement – here are some of the very best...

Dennis Viollet
1953 – 1962

Dennis Viollet is sometimes referred to as one of Manchester United's forgotten men. His star was shining at a tragic time for the Reds and his exploits were understandably overshadowed by other events, but this gifted inside forward is worthy of being labelled a Manchester United legend.

His record of almost two goals every three games is phenomenal, and we can only wonder what he might have achieved but for the Munich air disaster that Viollet escaped from relatively unscathed physically – the mental toll of such an horrific accident, however, can only be guessed at.

GAMES and GOALS

League	259	159
FA Cup	18	5
League Cup	2	1
Europe	12	13
Other	2	1
Total	**293**	**179**

TROPHIES

First Division x 2
FA Charity Shield x 2

One of the most underrated footballers
in the club's history.

BILL FOULKES

In all my years of playing football, never did I
come across such a quick-thinking player.
He was a truly magnificent player.

STANLEY MATTHEWS

Dennis Viollet was like a ghost with cannonballs in his shooting boots!

JIMMY MURPHY

Dennis was a remarkable player, a goal-scorer supreme... a pure footballer!

TOM FINNEY

Ryan Giggs
1990 – 2014

Where do you begin with a player like Ryan Giggs? Not since George Best did a player excite with a natural talent than only comes along once in a generation. Giggs had one thing many mercurial footballers didn't – longevity – and for 24 years this gifted winger tormented defences for the Reds with his trickery, skill and speed.

A Premier League great, he would spend his entire career at Old Trafford, clocking up a record amount of appearances and assists in the process. His influence on the most successful United side of all time cannot be understated and his astonishing 35 trophies won is unlikely to ever be beaten.

GAMES and GOALS

League 672 114
FA Cup..................... 74 12
League Cup 41 12
Europe....................157 29
Other 19 1
Total................. **963** **168**

TROPHIES

Premier League x 13
FA Cup x 4
League Cup x 4
FA Charity/Community Shield x 9

Champions League x 2
UEFA Super Cup x 1
Intercontinental Cup x 1
FIFA Club World Cup x 1

The first time I saw Giggsy, he was playing for Salford Boys against United's apprentices. He was thin and wiry, but he just glided past four of our apprentices as if they weren't even there, then he put the ball in the back of the net. I just thought, This kid's an absolute natural.

BRYAN ROBSON

Maybe one day people will say I was another Ryan Giggs.

GEORGE BEST

I have always considered myself to be very fortunate. To play for the biggest club in the world, which also happens to be the team I supported as a boy, means I have never had to consider changing away from Manchester United.

RYAN GIGGS

There's never been completion in my football career because I've always been striving for that next thing. You listen to people who have finished, and nothing replaces playing, but I'm still excited about not having to put my body through what I've put it through. And not feeling the disappointment that I feel.

RYAN GIGGS

Eric Cantona

1992 – 1997

Few players have had quite the impact Eric Cantona did during his five unforgettable years at Old Trafford. The nomadic Frenchman with the questionable temperament was a virtual unknown until he joined Leeds United, where he became an immediate cult hero, helping them to the league title in his only full season. Sir Alex Ferguson saw something other than trouble in Cantona, however – he believed him to be the missing piece of his jigsaw, and he was right. The magical Cantona found his spiritual home at Old Trafford and enjoyed his best years with the Reds during a magical five-year spell filled with brilliance and explosive moments – becoming one of the most popular players of all time to wear the red shirt in the process.

GAMES and GOALS

League	143	64
FA Cup	17	10
League Cup	6	1
Europe	16	5
Other	3	2
Total	**185**	**82**

TROPHIES

Premier League x 4
FA Cup x 2
FA Charity Shield x 3

I think he's right up there with the very best players who have played for Manchester United. He had this presence, and he could do things extra special when it was needed in those big games – that's why he did so well.

BRYAN ROBSON

I play with passion and fire. I have to accept that sometimes this fire does harm.

ERIC CANTONA

If ever there was one player, anywhere in the world, that was made for Manchester United, it was Cantona. He swaggered in, stuck his chest out, raised his head and surveyed everything as though he were asking: 'I'm Cantona. How big are you? Are you big enough for me?' But I do admit that there was something, perhaps a mental block, that stopped him from being the best player in the world. There was an element in his nature that seemed to prevent him from realising the full potential of his incredible gifts.

SIR ALEX FERGUSON

My best moment? I have a lot of good moments but the one I prefer is when I kicked the hooligan.

ERIC CANTONA

On his kung fu kick at a Crystal Palace fan in 1995

Andy Cole

1995 – 2001

It is more than coincidence that Manchester United won the Premier League title in five of the six seasons Andy Cole was at the club. A goal-scoring phenomenon at Newcastle, the Reds broke the British transfer record to buy the player they felt was a traditional No.9 and a goal poacher.

Cole settled in immediately at Old Trafford and, along with Eric Cantona and then Dwight Yorke, enhanced an already potent attack. Cole's critics claimed he needed at least three chances to score one goal, but he scored more than enough for United and played his part in winning nine major titles during his six years with the Reds.

GAMES and GOALS

League	195	93
FA Cup	21	9
League Cup	2	0
Europe	50	19
Other	7	0
Total	**275**	**121**

TROPHIES

Premier League x 5

FA Cup x 2

FA Charity Shield x 1

Champions League x 1

With Andy Cole up front they can score at any time. We'll be watching him very closely.

LAURENT ROBERT
Newcastle United player

[Andy Cole] was fantastic from day one.

SIR ALEX FERGUSON

United should have won more than three European Cups. When you look back at some of those semi-final and quarter-final defeats, we could and should have gone on to win the competition.

ANDY COLE

Of course, not everyone's going to get on but when you crossed that white line it didn't matter. For those 90 minutes it didn't matter what else was going on, we'd do anything to win.

ANDY COLE

Wayne Rooney

2004 – 2017

A true Manchester United great, Wayne Rooney spent the majority of his career with the Reds, giving the club his best years and becoming a legend in the process.

After becoming the world's most expensive teenager when he joined United from Everton in 2004, Rooney's potential became reality with better players around him and a manager who knew how to get the best out of him. He managed double figures in goals for all but his final season at Old Trafford and left as the Reds' all-time top goal-scorer. A powerful and skilful forward, Rooney also became an England legend during a glorious career for club and country.

GAMES and GOALS

League	393	183
FA Cup	40	22
League Cup	20	5
Europe	98	39
Other	8	4
Total	**559**	**253**

TROPHIES

Premier League x 5
FA Cup x 1
League Cup x 3
FA Community Shield x 4

Champions League x 1
Europa League x 1
FIFA Club World Cup x 1

I am very excited. I think we have got the best young player this country has seen in the past 30 years.

SIR ALEX FERGUSON

I obviously cannot deny that I am disappointed that I now don't hold this record. However, I am absolutely delighted that it is Wayne, as captain of my beloved club and country, who now holds this record.

SIR BOBBY ROBERT

On Rooney breaking his scoring record

Growing up, watching the Premier League as far back as I can remember, feeling the trophy and having the medal around my neck was an unbelievable feeling.

WAYNE ROONEY

The fans have been brilliant with me since I arrived and it's up to me through my performances to win them over again.

WAYNE ROONEY

Mark Hughes

1983 – 1986 and 1988 – 1995

Powerful, tenacious and blessed with the ability to score spectacular goals, Mark Hughes was not your average forward. The Wrexham-born Hughes joined United as a teenager and made an immediate impact in his first season – enough to make 55 appearances in his second year.

Nicknamed "Sparky", Hughes would join Barcelona aged 23 but struggled in Spain. After a year's loan at Bayern Munich, he returned to United, where he enjoyed seven more seasons, playing the best football of his career. A warrior of a player and a wonderful club servant.

GAMES and GOALS

League	345	120
FA Cup	46	17
League Cup	38	16
Europe	33	9
Other	5	1
Total	**467**	**163**

TROPHIES

Premier League x 2

FA Cup x 3

League Cup x 1

FA Charity Shield x 3

European Cup Winners' Cup x 1

UEFA Super Cup x 1

I don't think there's anyone who plays against him who can put their hand on their heart and say they enjoyed it.

GRAEME SOUNESS

Mark is a warrior with whom you could trust your life.

SIR ALEX FERGUSON

They say that pace is the first thing to go, but my game was never based on pace. It was about strength and power and withstanding challenges and getting in the right position.

MARK HUGHES

I always wanted to win, but I only used to get upset if I hadn't done myself and the people around me proud – that was my motivation for always wanting to do better.

MARK HUGHES

Bobby Charlton
1956 – 1973

If not the greatest player to ever represent Manchester United, he is pretty close! Bobby Charlton was a fantastic footballer who graced Old Trafford for 17 incredible seasons. A survivor of the Munich air disaster, Charlton loved and breathed United and would be a deciding factor in so many big games.

Captain of the 1968 European Cup winning side, Charlton was blessed with a thunderbolt shot, probably scoring more long range goals than anyone else – as he did for England, with whom he was integral to the 1966 World Cup triumph. His influence on the club is immeasurable and his incredible stats are testament to what a magnificent and loyal servant Charlton was.

GAMES and GOALS

League	606	199
FA Cup	78	19
League Cup	24	7
Europe	45	22
Other	5	2
Total	**758**	**249**

TROPHIES

First Division x 3

FA Cup x 1

FA Charity Shield x 2

European Cup x 1

There has never been a more popular footballer.
He was as near perfection as man and player
as it is possible to be.

SIR MATT BUSBY

Bobby Charlton was known for his creativity.
He was on the move for 90 minutes and had
the lungs of a horse.

FRANZ BECKENBAUER

Some people tell me that we professional players are soccer slaves. Well, if this is slavery, give me a life sentence.

SIR BOBBY CHARLTON

Success is not just about winning trophies, but about making a positive impact on and off the field.

SIR BOBBY CHARLTON

George Best
1963 – 1974

The young kid from Northern Ireland with magic in his boots, George Best was one of the most naturally gifted footballers to play for Manchester United. Deployed most often as a winger, Best could destroy teams almost single-handedly with his mesmeric dribbling ability and outrageous trickery.

A genuine crowd-pleaser, Best ultimately became a victim of his own success. His off-field issues gradually began to affect his performances on it, but when he was at his peak, Best was a breathtaking talent and perhaps isn't given the credit he deserved for the hard work he did to become one of the very best of all time.

GAMES and GOALS

League	361	137
FA Cup	46	21
League Cup	25	9
Europe	34	11
Other	4	1
Total	**470**	**179**

TROPHIES

First Division x 2

FA Charity Shield x 2

European Cup x 1

Players like George Best never die. What they leave behind them never dies.

JOSÉ MOURINHO

George was gifted with more individual ability than I had ever seen in a player. When you remember great names like Stanley Matthews and Tom Finney, I can't think of one who took the ball so close to an opponent to beat him with it as Best did.

SIR MATT BUSBY

That thing about being an icon, the fifth Beatle, I just found it so freaky.

GEORGE BEST

I used to dream about taking the ball round the keeper, stopping it on the line and then getting on my hands and knees and heading it into the net. When I scored against Benfica in the 1968 European Cup final I nearly did it. I left the keeper for dead but then I chickened out. I might have given the boss a heart attack!

GEORGE BEST

Denis Law
1962 – 1973

The man they called "The King" and possibly Manchester United's greatest natural goal-scorer, Denis Law was part of a Reds triumvirate that also included George Best and Bobby Charlton. Law topped 20 goals in a season on six occasions during his 11 years at Old Trafford. He also scored 18 hat-tricks, a club record that still stands.

With his spiky haircut and mullet, Law cut an instantly recognisable figure during his time with the club. He would prowl the box for half-chances, back post tap-ins and regularly finish off great moves. He was a predator, an instinctive striker with only Bobby Charlton and Wayne Rooney scoring more than the 237 he managed. A true United legend.

GAMES and GOALS

League	309	171
FA Cup	46	34
League Cup	11	3
Europe	35	28
Other	3	1
Total	**404**	**237**

TROPHIES

First Division x 2

FA Cup x 1

FA Charity Shield x 2

European Cup x 1

When I signed Denis I knew that we had the most exciting player in the game. He was the quickest-thinking player I ever saw, seconds quicker than anyone else. He had the most tremendous acceleration and could leap to enormous heights to head the ball with almost unbelievable accuracy and often the power of a shot. He had the courage to take on the biggest and most ferocious of opponents and his passing was impeccable.

SIR MATT BUSBY

The public absolutely loved him. They couldn't take their eyes off him. When the ball went into a position where Denis might be there to put it in the net, the fans would step forward in anticipation.

SIR BOBBY CHARLTON

The great part of playing with Bobby and George was that if one of us was having a bad day, the other two knew and that's what made our relationship special.

DENIS LAW

Reflecting on the what made the United Trilogy special

There were so many great players in action at that time, especially at Real Madrid, it's difficult to explain how I felt at being told I was joining the list of winners. I can't even say it was a dream come true, because I could never have dreamed of such a thing... Maybe there was a mistake in the mathematics.

DENIS LAW

On being awarded the Ballon d'Or in 1964

163

Ruud van Nistelrooy

2001 – 2006

Ruud van Nistelrooy was an astute signing by Sir Alex Ferguson. The Dutch striker had been prolific for PSV Eindhoven and was courted by many of Europe's top clubs, but he chose Old Trafford as his destination, and it proved to be a wise one. Van Nistelrooy would bag 150 goals in just 219 appearances for the Reds, becoming a huge crowd favourite in the process.

Though his stay with United didn't yield the silverware of the seasons just before or just after, the Netherlands international's time in Manchester was impactful and his stats ensure he is among the best strikers to ever play for the club.

GAMES and GOALS

League	150	95
FA Cup	14	14
League Cup	6	2
Europe	47	38
Other	2	1
Total	**219**	**150**

TROPHIES

Premier League x 1
FA Cup x 1
League Cup x 1
FA Community Shield x 1

Ruud van Nistelrooy has been the best – without doubt the best – finisher we have ever had at this club. We have had some brilliant centre forwards at United. But Van Nistelrooy has been the best, absolutely the best finisher.

SIR ALEX FERGUSON

Ruud van Nistelrooy was brilliant. Ruud was the best finisher, ever, but especially in one on one situations, just the keeper to beat. When Ruud was going through one on one, I never doubted him. Some players would be going, '******* hell – hard and low? Or dink it over?', but when Ruud was through there might as well have been no goalkeeper.

ROY KEANE

When it comes to losing with United, I feel solely responsible for it. I can't help it. My brain will work like mad after a defeat. I want to know where I have made the wrong decisions, how I could have changed things for this fantastic club.

RUUD VAN NISTELROOY

Of course I have the odd bad game like other players. But I can't accept that. Especially when things don't go right for United. It all means so much to me to be successful here. It drives me crazy at times.

RUUD VAN NISTELROOY

Cristiano Ronaldo

2003 – 2009 and 2021 – 2022

Perhaps – with Lionel Messi – the most famous footballer ever, Cristiano Ronaldo's magnificent career has been bookended by two spells with Manchester United.

He arrived as a teenager and took the Premier League by storm, the Portuguese forward who could do it all – dribble, head and score incredible goals – he thrilled fans at Old Trafford for six seasons before moving to Real Madrid and leaving some wonderful memories behind. Ronaldo returned to play for the Reds one more time, with less success, but without diluting his legacy. An exciting, generational talent who keeps United close to his heart.

GAMES and GOALS

League	236	103
FA Cup	26	13
League Cup	12	4
Europe	68	24
Other	3	1
Total	**346**	**145**

TROPHIES

Premier League x 3
FA Cup x 1
League Cup x 2
FA Community Shield x 1

Champions League x 1
FIFA Club World Cup x 1

Cristiano Ronaldo's first United game as a substitute was undoubtedly the most exciting debut performance I've ever seen.

GEORGE BEST

Scoring goals is the hardest part of the game. Some players don't even score in training! What more can you say about him? He's a genius!

ROY KEANE

The high point of my career was winning the Champions League. No one will ever erase that from my memory, in the same way that no one will ever erase the fact that I did it in a Manchester United shirt.

CRISTIANO RONALDO

People have to understand one thing: at the age of 18 I arrived at a dream club like Manchester United. It was a dream come true. But, even at that moment, I was thinking about playing in England for some years and then going to play in Spain. Even at that time I was thinking that way, and I always gave 100 per cent to everything.

CRISTIANO RONALDO

CHAPTER
5

THE GREATEST MANAGERS

Manchester United has had many good managers – but also some truly magnificent leaders who have left their mark not only on the domestic game but are world renowned for their incredible exploits.

In chronological order, here are four bosses who left their mark in one way or another at Old Trafford...

Ernest Mangnall
1903 – 1912

Ernest Mangnall was a unique manager in many ways and one of the most influential ever in the history of Manchester football. Despite being in charge of a Burnley side that had finished bottom of the Football League, Mangnall was given the job as United boss in 1903. He had very set ideas on how players should train and behave, as well as how a club should be run, but it was the influx of several Manchester City players – including superstar Billy Meredith – that helped Mangnall really put the Reds on the map.

Under his tenure, Mangnall delivered two First Division titles, the FA Cup and two FA Charity Shields as well as overseeing the move to Old Trafford before he left for Manchester City in 1912.

MANAGERIAL STATS

	PLD	W	D	L
League	331	179	66	86
FA Cup	36	19	9	8
League Cup	0	0	0	0
Europe	0	0	0	0
Other	3	2	1	0
Totals	**370**	**200**	**76**	**94**

TROPHIES

First Division x 2
FA Cup x 1
FA Charity Shield x 2

United not only won the league title for the first time, but also did so with a record number of points. Such facts speak volumes for the players, and for the management of Mr Ernest Mangnall.

THE ATHLETIC NEWS

It is not good, he considers, to give the men too much practice with the ball. Some people seemed to think players should have the ball every day, but once a week was plenty in his estimation. He believes in handling them as men, and finds he can get more work out of them by such a policy, accompanied with tact, than otherwise.

LANCASHIRE EVENING POST

Did you know?

After gaining promotion
from the Second Division in 1906,
Mangnall led United to their first
league title, winning the First
Division in 1908, followed by their
first FA Charity Shield win.

The following year he led
Manchester United to their first
FA Cup win.

Sir Matt Busby
1945 – 1969

Sir Matt Busby is one of the Manchester United's greatest managers of all time – for many, the best. Busby spent much of his playing career with Manchester City but grasped the opportunity to manage the Reds in 1945. His first success came with the FA Cup in 1948, but Busby was beginning to fashion an exciting young team that would result in the league title in 1951/52. By the mid-fifties, the "Busby Babes" were dominating English football with two more top flight titles.

Tragedy struck in 1958 when many of the Babes were killed during the Munich air disaster, Busby survived and would somehow rebuild his team, and two more titles would follow in the 1960s followed by the Holy Grail – the European Cup – in 1968.

MANAGERIAL STATS

	PLD	W	D	L
League	971	480	230	261
FA Cup	100	58	20	22
League Cup	4	1	1	2
Europe	56	34	11	11
Other	9	3	3	3
Totals	**1,140**	**576**	**265**	**299**

TROPHIES

First Division x 5

FA Cup x 2

FA Charity Shield x 5

European Cup x 1

He always told us that football is more than a game. It has the power to bring happiness to ordinary people. In the sadness and the rain, that belief was the glory of the life that had just ended — and the unbreakable pride I felt at being part of it. He *was* Manchester United.

SIR BOBBY CHARLTON

I played with some marvellous players at Manchester United and a great manager in Sir Matt Busby. When you think after the crash, Sir Matt lifting the European Cup at Wembley was just wonderful for everybody. It was lovely for Sir Matt Busby to win that trophy.

DENIS LAW

I never wanted Manchester United to be second to anybody. Only the best would be good enough.

SIR MATT BUSBY

At Manchester United we strive for perfection and if we fail we might just have to settle for excellence.

SIR MATT BUSBY

Tommy Docherty
1972 – 1977

One of Manchester United's most colourful managers, Tommy Docherty took on an ageing Reds side in 1972. Despite managing to keep the club up in his first season, his second ended in relegation. But the irrepressible Scot would rebuild a United side in his image, and after what was actually an entertaining one-year stint in the second tier, Docherty's United emerged with verve and energy and he would guide his team to successive FA Cup finals – the first a loss in 1976, the second an unforgettable triumph in 1977.

The Doc's personal life, however, did him no favours with the United board and he was sacked not long after, leaving many to wonder what he might have achieved had he stayed on.

MANAGERIAL STATS

	PLD	W	D	L
League	188	84	49	55
FA Cup	19	12	3	4
League Cup	17	9	4	4
Europe	4	2	0	2
Other	0	0	0	0
Totals	**228**	**107**	**56**	**65**

TROPHIES

Second Division x 1

FA Cup x 1

He could make anybody laugh. In the dressing room, an hour from kick off, he would entertain you from 2pm... and as a result players relaxed.

LOU MACARI

Tommy just said, 'We are going to come straight back,' and we'd come back in the right way, playing proper United, attacking, adventurous football and scoring plenty of goals.

SAMMY McILROY

I've always said there's a place for the press,
but they haven't dug it yet.

TOMMY DOCHERTY

I have more clubs than Jack Nicklaus!

TOMMY DOCHERTY

Sir Alex Ferguson
1986 – 2013

If Sir Matt Busby is the godfather of Manchester United, Sir Alex Ferguson is surely the GOAT – greatest of all time. The former Aberdeen boss joined the Reds in 1986 and after four unsuccessful seasons was perhaps one game away from the sack before he guided the Reds to 1990 FA Cup glory. The rest, as they say, is history, with the brilliant, fiery Scot overseeing two incredible eras of success at Old Trafford. During a peerless 27-year stint as boss, United won every trophy possible, played thrilling football and dominated the English and European game.

It's with a fair degree of certainty that Sir Alex's achievements will never be repeated again, not only at United, but by any team in England.

MANAGERIAL STATS

	PLD	W	D	L
League	1,035	625	238	172
FA Cup	120	80	22	18
League Cup	97	62	10	25
Europe	223	119	60	44
Other	25	9	8	8
Totals	**1,500**	**895**	**338**	**267**

TROPHIES

Premier League x 13
FA Cup x 5
League Cup x 4
FA Charity/Community Shield x 10

Champions League x 2
European Cup Winners' Cup x 1
UEFA Super Cup x 1
Intercontinental Cup x 1
FIFA Club World Cup x 1

Manchester United are one of the best teams in the world and have been for a long time. That is because Sir Alex Ferguson has maintained winning trophies at the same time as creating outstanding teams. That is an art, and I only have respect for him and what he has achieved. He is one of the best of all time.

PEP GUARDIOLA

You may find another Beckham or Ronaldo, but never ever will you find another Sir Alex Ferguson.

ERIC CANTONA

At the end of this game, the European Cup will be only six feet away from you, and you'll not even be able to touch it if we lose. And for many of you, that will be the closest you will ever get. Don't you dare come back in here without giving your all.

SIR ALEX FERGUSON

I'm privileged to have followed Sir Matt because all you have to do is to try and maintain the standards that he set so many years ago.

SIR ALEX FERGUSON

Appearance records

as of 31/01/2025

Most appearances in all competitions:
Ryan Giggs, 963

Most appearances as a goalkeeper:
David de Gea, 545

Most league appearances: **Ryan Giggs, 672**

Most FA Cup appearances:
Bobby Charlton, 78

Most European appearances:
Ryan Giggs, 157

Most consecutive appearances:
Steve Coppell, 206
from 15 January 1977 to 7 November 1981

Youngest first-team player:
David Gaskell, 16 years, 19 days
against Manchester City, Charity Shield, 24 October 1956

Oldest first-team player:
Billy Meredith, 46 years, 281 days
against Derby County, First Division, 7 May 1921

Goal-scoring records

as of 31/01/2025

Record goal-scorer: **Wayne Rooney, 253**

Most goals in a season: **Denis Law, 46**
in the 1963–64 season

Most league goals in a season:
Dennis Viollet, 32
in the First Division, 1959–60

Most FA Cup goals: **Denis Law, 34**

Most European goals: **Wayne Rooney, 39**

Fastest goal scored in a match:
Bryan Robson, 12 seconds
against Burnley, League Cup second round, 26 September 1984

Most hat-tricks: **Denis Law, 18**

Youngest goal-scorer:
Norman Whiteside, 17 years, 8 days
against Stoke City, First Division, 15 May 1982

Oldest goal-scorer:
Ryan Giggs, 39 years, 87 days
against Queens Park Rangers, Premier League, 23 February 2013

The Theatre of Dreams

The nickname of Old Trafford, the home of Manchester United's legends